Famous
Chess Players

Bobby Fischer plays many games at once during an exhibition of simultaneous chess in 1964.

A Pull Ahead Book

Famous Chess Players

Peter Morris Lerner

 Lerner Publications Company • Minneapolis, Minnesota

ACKNOWLEDGMENTS: The illustrations are reproduced through the courtesy of: pp. 2, 56, 61, 64, 72, Art Zeller; pp. 5, 13, 22, 24, 26, 29, 31, 36, 39, 40, 45, 46, 49, 78, 84, United Press International; pp. 6, 16, 20, Independent Picture Service; p. 8, The Metropolitan Museum of Art, Harris Brisbane Dick Fund, 1943; p. 10, Mark Gray; p. 14, The Metropolitan Museum of Art, Gift of Gustavus A. Pfeiffer, 1948; pp. 32, 50, 55, 62, 66, 69, 70, 75, Sovfoto; p. 76, Wide World Photos.

Back Cover: Art Zeller.

LIBRARY OF CONGRESS CATALOGING IN PUBLICATION DATA

Lerner, Peter Morris.
  Famous chess players.

    (A Pull Ahead Book)
    CONTENTS: Harry N. Pillsbury—Emanuel Lasker—José R. Capablanca. [etc.]

    1. Chess—Biography—Juvenile literature. [1. Chess—Biography] I. Title.

  GV1438.L47   794.1′092′2 [920]   72-3593
  ISBN 0-8225-0466-9

International Standard Book Number: 0-8225-0466-9
Library of Congress Catalog Card Number: 72-3593

contents

Chess champion José Capablanca at an exhibition of simultaneous chess, 1921

This painting on the tomb of an Egyptian queen shows the queen playing a game very similar to chess.

Introduction

People have been playing chess for almost 1,500 years. Most authorities believe that the game originated in India during the 6th century A.D. It was probably invented by a philosopher who wanted to represent a battle between two Indian armies. In India, battles used to be decided by the death or capture of the king, and this tradition was transferred to the chessboard.

Chess spread westward from India to Persia (Iran) in the 6th century. After the Arabs conquered Persia in the 600s, the game spread throughout the Moslem world. By the 8th century the game had spread eastward from India to China, and by the 11th century, farther eastward to Korea and Japan.

Chess reached Europe in the 11th century by way of the Moslem world. The Arabs brought the game with them to Spain by way of North Africa, and to Italy via the trade routes across the Mediterranean Sea.

This woodcut is from the title page of a book printed in Italy during the 15th century. Chess became very popular in Italy during the 16th and 17th centuries. (*Courtesy The Metropolitan Museum of Art*)

Italy and Spain were the most important centers of chess during the 16th and 17th centuries. During the 18th century, chess supremacy passed to England and France. Germany fielded the strongest players in the late 19th century, and Russia has dominated the game since the 1930s. However, the victory of America's Bobby Fischer over Russia's Boris Spassky in the 1972 World Chess Championship may mark the end of Soviet dominance of the chess world.

The game of chess is played on a checkered board by two players. The 64-square board used in chess is the same as that used in checkers. The 32 light-colored squares make up the "white" side; the 32 dark-colored squares, the "black" side. Each player starts the game with a set of 16 chessmen: eight pawns (the lowest ranking chessmen), two knights, two bishops, two rooks (or castles), one queen (the most powerful piece on the board), and one king (the most important piece on the board). The chessmen are light in color for the white side, and dark in color for the black side.

Each type of chessman is moved according to specific rules. These rules, along with the names and shapes of the chessmen, have undergone many changes through the years. But whenever and wherever chess is played, the object of the game is to force the surrender of the opponent's king. Each player works toward this goal by eliminating his opponent's chessmen, or material. A chessman is said to be captured when it is displaced by the move of an opposing chessman into its square. Once a chessman has been captured, it is removed from the board.

A contemporary chess set showing the opening positions of the pieces

A chess game is usually divided into three parts: the opening, the middle game, and the endgame. The opening consists of the series of moves made by each player at the beginning of the game. A number of books have been written on the theories behind the opening, and most experienced players know the first 10 to 15 moves of many opening strategies by heart. The middle game takes place after most of the chessmen have been moved from their original squares. During the middle game a player is away from theory and on his own. He must use his imagination and good judgment to attack and defend. Once the number of pieces on the board has been greatly reduced, the endgame, or final stage of the game, is played. During the endgame, each player attempts to convert his material or positional advantages into a win.

Chess players use various methods to achieve a victory. One way is through direct assault upon the opponent's king. It is here that a player sacrifices pieces for the sake of setting up the attack. The game is over when a king is checkmated; that is, when the king is under attack and has no safe square into which he can move. If the checkmate succeeds, the attacker wins. But if the opponent can protect his king and hold onto his extra chessmen through effective counterplay, he may triumph in the end. If neither player is able to checkmate the other's king, the result is said to be a drawn game.

Attacks directed at the opponent's king are appealing to the average chess player, but there are safer, less risky methods of winning. When a player builds up pressure on weak or unprotected squares, the name of the game is positional chess. Once a player wins a positional advantage, he can usually capture a number of his opponent's chessmen. And when the opponent falls hopelessly behind in material, he will usually resign because he will be unable to protect his king from the inevitable mating attack.

The techniques of chess players often vary. For example, one player might play speculatively. That is, the player recognizes that his general plan is unsound, but he hopes to confuse and bewilder his opponent. Another player may be more methodical. Avoiding risks and complications, he tries to convert the smallest advantage into a victory. Some chess players hope to create something new every time they sit down at the chessboard. They experiment with new moves and ideas in the opening, trying to get their opponent away from theory and books.

Chess is played competitively at all ages and at all levels of ability. There are open tournaments in which everyone is eligible, tournaments restricted to high school and junior high school students, and those in which only one opponent is invited to compete. The scoring system used in chess competitions is quite simple. A win counts for one point, a draw for half a point, and a loss for nothing. The player with the most points at the end of a chess tournament is the winner.

The highest rank one can earn in chess is grandmaster. This title is achieved by accumulating a particular number of points in international tournaments. Of the 25,000 members in the United States Chess Federation, only 11 are grandmasters. Of these, eight were born in the United States.

Chess is a game for people of all ages. The youngsters in this photo are playing the game with a set made out of nuts and bolts.

The International Chess Federation is the most important chess organization in the world. Established in 1924, it includes the official chess federations of over 40 countries. In addition to interpreting the rules of chess, the organization governs the series of tournaments leading up to the World Championship. First, zonal tournaments are held throughout the various chess zones of the world. The winners of the zonal tournaments then participate in an Interzonal Tournament. Next, the finalists of the Interzonal Tournament participate in the Candidates' Tournament. And finally, the winner of the Candidates' Tournament plays against the World Champion in the World Chess Championship.

This interesting chess set comes from Japan, where chess is very popular (*Courtesy The Metropolitan Museum of Art*)

Millions of people have played chess through the years, but only a few of them have been outstanding. In this book, 12 of the greatest chess players of the 19th and 20th centuries are brought together. The social, ethnic, and religious backgrounds of these players are as different as the countries they come from. Some of the players mastered chess when they were children; others did not learn the game until they were older. Some of them have had interests outside of chess, while for others, chess has been their entire life.

In spite of these differences, the players discussed in this book have many things in common. They have all displayed some special qualities that have put them at the top. They have all possessed a great will to win and a tremendous amount of self-confidence. These chess masters have frequently preferred to risk defeat rather than to accept a draw. All have put an enormous amount of work and study into the game of chess. But work alone does not make a great chess player. The chess greats have not been satisfied with the ordinary. All of the "number ones" have had fine intuition, and all have been capable of grasping concepts and making moves unimaginable to the average chess player. In the following pages, you will read about 12 champion chess players who have met the challenge of the board and mastered the game, each in his own way.

Harry N. Pillsbury

Harry N. Pillsbury
(1872-1906)

Harry Pillsbury was born in Somerville, Massachusetts, on December 5, 1872. He did not learn to play chess until 1888, when he was 16. Pillsbury mastered his game at the Boston Young Men's Christian Union and the Deschapelles Chess and Whist Club. In the years that followed, he built up his reputation as one of the finest chess players of all time.

In 1895 Pillsbury played in the great Hastings Tournament in England. He came as an unknown and lost his first game. People thought he was through. But after his initial failure, Pillsbury bounced back, winning game after game. He took first place in the important tournament and won $1,200. Pillsbury beat Emanuel Lasker (then the World Chess Champion), as well as the leading players of Austria, France, Germany, Italy, and Russia.

Pillsbury never again had a success equal to the one at Hastings, but he continued to play well in most of his later tournaments. Between 1895 and 1905 the supreme tournament player was Emanuel Lasker of Germany. But in the individual matches between Lasker and Pillsbury, the two were equal.

During the many periods when Pillsbury was affected by ill health, his playing suffered. But when he performed at his best, he had no superior. In 1897, at the age of 25, Pillsbury entered the United States Chess Championship. He won the event by defeating former champion Jackson W. Showalter. Pillsbury held the U.S. title until his death in 1906.

Pillsbury's superb memory made him one of the finest players of blindfold chess in the history of the game. Pillsbury was also considered to be one of the top checker players in the United States. He could play a dozen games of chess, six games of checkers, and a hand of whist simultaneously. At any time during an exhibition, Pillsbury could repeat all the moves made on every board and even correct possible errors made by his scorers.

On one occasion, Pillsbury was given a memory test just before taking on 20 chess opponents simultaneously. He was shown the following list of long and unusual words: antiphlogistine, periosteum, takadiastase, plasman, ambrosia, Threlkeld, streptococcus, micrococcus, plasmodium, Mississippi, Freiheit, Philadelphia, Cincinnati, athletics, no war, Etchenberg, American, Russian, philosophy, Piet Potgelter's Rost, salama gundi, oomisillecoosti, Bangmamvate, Schlechter's Nek, Maninyama, theosophy, catechism, and Madjesoomalops. Pillsbury studied the list, defeated his 20 opponents, and then repeated the words without a single mistake. To top it off, he recited the list backwards!

Harry Pillsbury died in 1906 at the age of 34. The tension generated during his exhibitions of blindfold chess, together with his constant smoking of cigars and general lack of physical care, may have played a part in his early death. Whatever the cause of Pillsbury's untimely death, he would long be remembered as one of the world's greatest chess players.

Emanuel Lasker

Emanuel Lasker
(1868-1941)

Emanuel Lasker was born on December 24, 1868, in Berlinchen, Germany. He was the second son of the cantor (singer) at the local synagogue. At an early age, Lasker showed great skill in arithmetic, and at 11, he was sent to study in Berlin. There, his older brother taught him how to play chess. Young Lasker soon found that he could make small sums of money playing chess in a nearby cafe.

When Lasker was 20, he decided to give up his studies and make a career out of chess. This decision eventually paid off, for in 1894 Lasker claimed the title of World Chess Champion after defeating Austria's William Steinitz, the reigning titleholder. Lasker held the world chess title for 27 straight years—an incredible feat. Then, in 1921, he lost the title to José Capablanca of Cuba. Even after this defeat, Lasker continued to be an outstanding player.

Most chess players lose their creativity as they approach middle age. Not so with Lasker. Because of his remarkable intellectual powers, his ability to criticize himself, and his strong desire to acquire new knowledge, Lasker avoided all danger of turning into a mechanical chess player.

Emanuel Lasker (seated at the right) and Polish grandmaster Akiba Rubin-stein (standing behind Lasker) direct their moves in a human chess game at the Berlin Sports Palace in 1925.

Lasker was 56 years old when he had what was probably his greatest tournament success. He won an important chess tournament in New York in 1924, defeating World Champion José Capablanca and future World Champion Alexander Alekhine of Russia.

After finishing second in a Moscow tournament in 1925, Lasker became inactive for nine years. Time and again a rumor sprouted: "Lasker is coming out of retirement!" But he did not return to active competition until 1934, when he competed in the Grandmaster Tournament in Zurich, Switzerland. There, he defeated Max Euwe, challenger to World Champion Alexander Alekhine, in the first round.

Lasker was frequently not as well prepared in chess theory as his opponents, but he was an outstanding tactician. Falling into a lost position after the opening, he would hang on and pull out a victory. Lasker believed that chess was a struggle, and he played the man rather than the board. He did not always make the strongest move on the board, but he would make the move that disturbed his opponent the most. One reason that Lasker lost the World Championship to José Capablanca in 1921 was that Capablanca was not known to have any psychological or technical weaknesses that Lasker could exploit.

Emanuel Lasker (center) judging a chess game between Alexander Alekhine (left) and German grandmaster Ewfim Bogoljubov (right), 1929

Lasker was one of the few chess greats whose life was not centered on chess alone. In addition to being a chess genius, he also shone in philosophy and mathematics (he had a doctorate in the latter subject). Albert Einstein, the brilliant scientist who advanced the theory of relativity, was one of Lasker's best friends.

The illness that led to Lasker's death in 1941 was diagnosed as uremic poisoning (a kidney ailment), but those who knew him said that Lasker was a victim of World War II. In order to avoid persecution by the Nazis, he fled from Germany in 1933. As a result, he was left with serious financial worries.

When Lasker died, chess lost not only one of its finest players, but also one of its finest minds. Although he cared little about opening theory, his determination and ability to win must mark Lasker as one of the finest chess players of all time.

José Capablanca preparing for an important chess tournament in 1932

José R. Capablanca

(1888-1942)

José Capablanca was born in Havana, Cuba, on November 19, 1888. His father and grandfather, who were officers in the Spanish army, played chess, and José learned the game at the age of four by watching them. José was no ordinary child. Most people look at the chessboard and see inanimate pieces of wood or plastic on different colored squares. Not José. He saw a human drama unfold every time he gazed at the board. At a glance, he could separate the strong positions from the weak ones. He also had the ability to figure out most moves before playing them. But, like other prodigies, he could not explain his gift.

When Capablanca was 12 years old, he astonished everyone by crushing the chess champion of Cuba in a 10-game match. Later, in New York City, he attended preparatory school and studied engineering at Columbia University. It was in New York that Capablanca developed the skill that someday would make him the World Chess Champion. To force himself to concentrate, he played thousands of games of skittle chess. (Skittle chess is played for pure enjoyment, and at a more leisurely rate than regular tournament chess. One tests new ideas in skittles to prepare oneself for tournaments.) By the time he was 18, Capablanca already was among the top chess players in the United States. In 1909 he defeated the current United States Champion, Frank J. Marshall, in an important match. Of the 23 games in the match, Capablanca won 8, lost 1, and drew 14.

Capablanca grew increasingly famous. People were intrigued by his name and his romantic Latin background. Even those who did not know how to play chess respected Capablanca and his accomplishments.

Capablanca during an exhibition of simultaneous chess, 1921

In 1911 Capablanca challenged World Champion Emanuel Lasker to a match for the world title. But because of World War I, Lasker was not able to accept until 1921. When the match was finally played, Capablanca won an easy victory. After losing four games Lasker conceded the match, claiming poor health. But he admitted that Capablanca was the better player.

From 1916 to 1924 Capablanca did not lose a single game of professional chess! During the 20 years from 1911 to 1931, he finished no lower than third place in all the tournaments in which he took part.

Capablanca's talent lay in his ability to avoid all that might complicate a situation. Although he did not experiment or invent a unique style, he achieved fantastic results. Capablanca could recognize the smallest danger and take advantage of the smallest mistake. Once he got an advantage, no matter how minute, his faultless technique never failed him. Capablanca was a master of simplification. When he found himself in a difficult position, he looked ahead, forced the exchange of several chessmen, and set up his men in a winning position. Unlike the great Russian player Alexander Alekhine, who concentrated on the openings, Capablanca's chief interest was in the endgames.

Capablanca held the title of World Chess Champion from 1921 to 1927. When Capablanca was matched against Alexander Alekhine in the 1927 World Chess Championship, most people expected him to retain his title. He lost the first game of the match, however, and the psychological shock was too much for him. As a result, Alexander Alekhine became the new World Chess Champion.

José Capablanca (left) meets with U.S. chess master Herman Steiner (right) for an informal game of chess in Los Angeles, 1933.

Until his death, Capablanca attempted to get a return match with Alekhine, but was unsuccessful. In 1941 he tried to arrange a match in the United States, but Alekhine was unable to leave Germany because of wartime difficulties in getting a passport. On March 7, 1942, José Capablanca died of a cerebral hemorrage at the Manhattan Chess Club.

Perhaps Emanuel Lasker summed up Capablanca's chess talents the best when he said, "I have known many chess players, but only one chess genius, Capablanca."

Alexander Alekhine

Alexander A. Alekhine
(1892-1946)

Alexander Alekhine was born in Moscow on November 1, 1892. His mother taught him how to play chess. Because he was from a wealthy family, he had a lot of time as a child to spend on the game. At the age of 12, Alexander was already playing correspondence chess by mail. Using school hours to study chess, he analyzed positions in his head because his teacher would not permit him to keep a board and set in class.

By the time he was 18, Alekhine had already taken part in an important chess tournament in Hamburg, Germany. In 1914 he tied for first place in the Russian Chess Championship. Next, Alekhine took third place in a tournament in St. Petersburg, coming in right behind Emanuel Lasker and José Capablanca—two of the greatest players of all time. These successes, especially the brilliant way in which he achieved them, made Alekhine the new hero of the chess world.

Alekhine was leading a tournament in Mannheim, Germany, when World War I broke out. Although Alekhine won the tournament, he lost his freedom—he and the other Russian players were held in Germany. After escaping from Germany, Alekhine returned to his native land to serve as a worker for the Red Cross division of the Russian army. When the Russian Revolution erupted in 1917, Alekhine was condemned to death by the Bolsheviks. He was later reprieved, however, and set free. In 1921 Alekhine left Russia to study law at the Sorbonne in Paris. Years later he became a naturalized citizen of France.

From 1921 to 1927 Alekhine won practically every tournament in which he played. Only the current World Champion, José Capablanca, and ex-World Champion Emanuel Lasker could restrain him. In 1927 Alekhine played a match with Capablanca in Buenos Aires, Argentina, for the World Championship. Alekhine captured the world title after winning 6 games, losing 3, and drawing 25.

Although Alekhine gave up smoking for the World Championship, he took up the habit again as soon as the match was completed. One night he went to bed with a lighted cigarette and woke up amid flames. Luckily, he was not injured.

In 1929 Alekhine easily retained his world title by defeating Ewfim Bogoljubov, a German grandmaster. Soon afterwards he participated in a tournament at San Remo, Italy, where he had what some consider his greatest triumph. Never was a chess player so near perfection. Alekhine's game was flawless and his winning percentage unbelievable. Europe's grandmasters played like children against him.

Alekhine worked at chess for eight hours every day. He was the only master of the time who took the openings so seriously. He would accept any difficulty, even prolonged manuevering of the knights, in order to get an advantage from the opening. Alekhine's greatness came from his attack strategy and from his ability to quickly develop his pieces, creating solid positions free of weaknesses.

In 1931 World Champion Alexander Alekhine refereed a transatlantic chess match in Paris. The match was conducted by cable between France and the United States.

After his victory at San Remo, Alekhine's performance changed. He turned from bold attacks to rash shortcuts, hastening into many unfavorable positions. If one can beat an opponent by one's genius, he reasoned, why waste a few extra hours winning a long positional game. After taking second place in a 1934 match at Hastings, England, Alekhine competed in a tournament at Zurich. He won the tournament but lost his individual match with Max Euwe, the Hollander who later challenged him for the world title. In the 1935 World Championship match with Euwe, Alekhine took an early lead. But, having underestimated his opponent and overindulged in alcohol, Alekhine lost his title to Euwe.

In 1937 Alekhine readied himself for a return match with Euwe. The Russian had regained his touch of years before, and he played brilliantly. Euwe, with his methodical approach, was overwhelmed by the complexities of the positions. Hence Alekhine easily regained the lost title.

Alexander Alekhine plays a game of chess
with his Siamese kitten, Chouette, 1936.

In 1941 great bitterness arose in many chess circles
because Alekhine supposedly wrote a series of articles in
which he attacked all the leading Jewish chess players,
including Emanuel Lasker, Mikhail Botvinnik, Samuel
Reshevsky, and Max Euwe. He even went so far as to blame
"Jewish influence" for the loss of his match to Euwe in
1935. Nevertheless, Alekhine maintained his popularity for
three years in Germany as well as in occupied Poland—
perhaps because many people who knew him thought the
anti-Jewish articles were a Nazi trick.

After World War II ended, Alekhine denied having
written against the Jews, but the damage had been done.
The idea of Alekhine's having been used as a puppet by the
Nazis was enough to make many fellow chess players
refuse to compete in tournaments in which Alekhine
planned to play.

In 1946 the Moscow Chess Club put up $10,000 to support a match for the world title between Alekhine and Mikhail Botvinnik (also a Russian). Most chess federations throughout the world decided to ignore the unproved charges that Alekhine had worked with the Nazis, and they endorsed the match.

On March 23, 1946, shortly before the scheduled match with Botvinnik, World Champion Alekhine died of a heart attack. After his death an editorial in the *New York Times* suggested that, putting aside charges of Nazi collaboration, and "looking only at Alekhine's career as a chess master, no other name, not in a thousand years, could be placed ahead of his. The question is can any be placed beside it?"

Chess champion Frank J. Marshall holds the Hamilton Russel Trophy awarded to him for his brilliance in chess, 1933.

Frank J. Marshall

(1877-1944)

Frank J. Marshall was born in New York on August 10, 1877. When he was eight years old, he moved with his parents and five brothers to Montreal. At the age of 10, Frank learned to play chess from his father. The elder Marshall soon realized that his son possessed a special talent for chess and sought stronger opposition for the boy. Frank joined the Montreal Chess Club and developed into one of the best players in the city. Opponents were astounded by his deep insight and aggressive playing.

In 1896 the Marshall family returned to New York, and Frank became one of the top players in the metropolitan area. He won the Junior Championship of the New York Chess Association in 1897. Two years later he won the championship of the Brooklyn Chess Club.

In 1899, as the representative of the Brooklyn and Manhattan chess clubs, Marshall traveled to London to take part in the International Tournament. But he was not allowed to play in the Masters Tournament because it already was too large. Instead, he was assigned to play a minor chess event, in which he took first place. Because of the outstanding quality of his games, chess devotees predicted that Marshall would be a future contender for the World Championship. A year later Marshall entered the International Masters Tournament in Paris. Although he finished in a tie for third place, he defeated the top two finishers—Emanuel Lasker of Germany and Harry Pillsbury of the United States.

After his excellent showing in Paris, Marshall competed whenever possible at international events. His uneven style of playing often made his final standing unpredictable; he might defeat the leaders but bow to the weaker players. Marshall's great love of chess kept him from playing for a draw, even when the first prize depended on it. He loved combinations—linked series of moves designed to win a more favorable position, gain material, or to achieve a checkmate. Marshall's combinations sometimes backfired, but more often than not, they spelled defeat for his opponents.

Marshall's finest triumph came in 1904 at the International Tournament in Cambridge Springs, Pennsylvania. He did not lose a single game, and he took first place by two points over a field of outstanding players that included Lasker and Pillsbury. The following year Marshall went to St. Louis to compete in the United States Chess Championship. To Marshall's disappointment, Pillsbury, the reigning champion, was too ill to compete. Although Marshall won the tournament, he said he would not accept the title of U.S. Champion until he had defeated Pillsbury in a match. Unfortunately, Pillsbury died before Marshall could arrange a match with him. Even though the chess world then considered Marshall the unquestioned U.S. Champion, Marshall refused to accept the title until he had defeated Jackson W. Showalter, a champion before Pillsbury.

During the years that followed, Marshall continued to distinguish himself as a champion chess player. In 1914 Nicholas II, the czar of Russia, conferred the title of "Grandmaster of Chess" on Marshall and the other top finishers in the St. Petersburg Tournament—Lasker, Capablanca, Alekhine, and the German physician Tarrasch. Then, in 1922, Marshall set a record by playing 155 games of chess simultaneously. He finished in seven hours with an average playing time of only three minutes a game! Marshall won 126 of the games, lost 8, and drew 21.

Marshall believed that chess consisted of bold combinations and calculated sacrifices, and his games provided excellent examples of sustained attacks. Few players possessed as much daring and originality as Marshall. Strongly opposed to stereotyped playing, he managed to create something new in almost every game. He was most dangerous when on the brink of defeat. In an almost hopeless position, he could set up a brilliant combination and turn an impending loss into a stunning victory.

Frank J. Marshall (left) plays a game of chess with Harold M. Phillips (right), a former New York State Chess Champion, 1936.

In 1936 Marshall retired as United States Chess Champion. He decided not to defend his title in order to spend more time helping younger players develop their chess talents. He had held the crown for 31 years—a feat which no one else has come close to approaching.

On November 9, 1944, Frank J. Marshall died suddenly of a heart attack. With Marshall's death, the world of chess lost one of its most creative and courageous players.

Vera Menchik competes in the Women's World Chess Championship in 1939.

Vera Menchik

(1906-1944)

On February 16, 1906, Vera Menchik was born in Moscow. Her father taught her to play chess at the age of nine. In 1921 her family moved to Hastings, England, and in 1923 Vera joined the Hastings Chess Club. There, veteran master Geza Maroczy showed her the finer points of the game.

Vera Menchik was the first woman ever to play in the British Chess Championship and the first to compete in a master tournament. In 1927 she won the Women's World Chess Championship with an unapproachable score of 10 wins and 1 draw. Menchik defended her title successfully in 1930, 1931, 1935, and 1939.

Chess champion Vera Menchik plays 20 opponents simultaneously in London, 1931.

In spite of Vera Menchik's long string of victories, many male chess players were unimpressed with her ability. The Viennese chess master Albert Becker suggested that any man who lost to Menchik should be made a member of the Menchik Club. Ironically, Becker promptly became the first member! Other chess greats who followed in Becker's footsteps were future World Champion Max Euwe and future U.S. Champion Samuel Reshevsky.

Menchik was purely a positional player, and she did not go out for risky combinative playing. She specialized in exploiting the weaknesses in her opponents' games. Few handled the endgame with more skill than she. Vera's only weakness might have been a lack of imagination. Her tournament results, however, have yet to be surpassed by another female chess player. In fact, Menchik was the only woman player who could hold her own against the strongest of male opponents.

World War II brought a tragic end to the career of the world's greatest female chess player. Vera Menchik, together with her mother and sister, was killed during a bomb attack in London on June 27, 1944.

Mikhail M. Botvinnik, 1970

Mikhail M. Botvinnik

(1911-   )

Mikhail Botvinnik was born on August 17, 1911, in what was then St. Petersburg, was later Petrograd, and today is Leningrad. He learned to play chess in 1924 at the age of 13. In the same year he joined the Leningrad Chess Club, even though the minimum age for membership was 16. A year later Botvinnik was one of four people to whom World Champion José Capablanca lost while giving an exhibition of simultaneous chess play. Capablanca said of Botvinnik, "He plays with the self-confidence of a master. He will go far."

At 16 Botvinnik became a sensation in Russia by tying for fifth place in the Soviet Chess Championship. During the next couple of years he concentrated on becoming an electrical engineer and gave little thought to chess. Botvinnik loved chess, but he never let it interfere with his studies.

In 1931 Botvinnik again participated in the Soviet Chess Championship. Although he lost the first game of the tournament, he went on to win the championship, scoring a full two points ahead of the field. Four years later Botvinnik tied with José Capablanca for first place in the famous Nottingham Tournament. Many consider that chess event the most spectacular of all time because of the large number of chess greats who participated in it. Besides Botvinnik and Capablanca, the players included Emanuel Lasker, Alexander Alekhine, Estonian grandmaster Paul Keres, and future U.S. Chess Champion Samuel Reshevsky.

In 1940 Botvinnik could do no better than tie for fifth place in the Soviet Chess Championship. But because two of the players tied for first place, a play-off was arranged among the top six finishers in the tournament. Winning the play-off was very important to Botvinnik: although he was only 30 years old at the time, many people thought he was all through as a chess player. It is said that no one ever trained harder for a chess event than Botvinnik did for the play-off. He ordered his trainer to blow smoke in his face during practice sessions in order to prepare himself to cope with the smoking habit of one of his opponents. All his hard training paid off, for Botvinnik won the play-off by two and a half points. Although he later became a World Chess Champion, Botvinnik considers his victory in the play-off his greatest triumph.

One of Botvinnik's best qualities has been his great perseverance. He knows how to maneuver and slowly improve his position while seizing every opportunity, no matter how small. His game has no weak points. Former World Champion Max Euwe once said, "Most players feel uncomfortable in difficult positions, but Botvinnik seems to enjoy them." Some of Botvinnik's combinations have run up to 20 moves. Although primarily a positional player, he is brilliant in attack.

	Botvinnik	Smyslov	Reshevsky	Keres	Euwe	Total
Botvinnik	————	½ ½ 1 ½ ½	1 ½ 0 1 1	1 1 1 1 0	1 ½ 1 ½ ½	14
Smyslov	½ ½ 0 ½ ½	————	½ ½ 1 ½ ½	0 0 ½ 1 ½	1 1 0 1 1	11
Reshevsky	0 ½ 1 0 0	½ ½ 0 ½ ½	————	1 ½ 0 1 ½	1 ½ ½ 1 1	10½
Keres	0 0 0 0 1	1 1 ½ 0 ½	0 ½ 1 0 ½	————	1 ½ 1 1 1	10½
Euwe	0 ½ 0 ½ ½	0 0 1 0 0	0 ½ ½ 0 0	0 ½ 0 0 0	————	4

This table shows the final scores for the 1948 World Chess Championship, which Mikhail Botvinnik won. Note that a win counts for one point, a draw for half a point, and a loss for nothing.

In 1948 Mikhail Botvinnik became World Chess Champion by taking first place in the tournament to determine a successor to Alexander Alekhine, who had died in 1946. Botvinnik retained the world title until 1957, when he lost it to Vassily Smyslov. In their rematch two years later, Botvinnik won the title back. He lost the title to Mikhail Tal in 1960, but then recaptured it again in 1961. Two years later Botvinnik lost the title, probably for good, to Russian grandmaster Tigran Petrosian. Although it is unlikely that Botvinnik will ever become World Champion again, he is still one of the brightest stars in the universe of chess.

Mikhail Botvinnik (right) lost his title to Tigran Petrosian (left) in the 1963 World Chess Championship.

Botvinnik has tried to program computers to play chess on the master level. So far, he has succeeded only in developing a program that enables the computer to perform at about the same strength as its average human counterpart. One of the problems involved is that there are more than 1,695,182,291,005,440,000,000,000,000,000 possibilities for the first 10 moves of chess! Will Botvinnik succeed? No one knows for sure. But most chess players hope he will not, because a successful computerized chess program could mark the end of chess as we know it.

In the early 1970s Botvinnik announced his retirement from chess. Nevertheless, some people still consider him the best chess player in the world today.

Samuel Reshevsky, 1966

Samuel Reshevsky
(1911-   )

On November 26, 1911, Samuel Reshevsky was born in the Polish village of Ozorkow. He was the sixth child of Orthodox Jewish parents. Sammy learned to play chess when he was only four years old. Initially, his participation had taken the form of interfering in his father's games by moving the pieces from square to square. Instead of getting upset, Sammy's father had taught him how to play the game.

Sammy learned to play chess so quickly and so well that in a few months he was beating everyone in his village. So he and his parents moved to Lodz, Poland, where the Polish master Salve tutored Sammy in chess. When Sammy was six he was taken to Warsaw, where he caused such a sensation that the great Polish grandmaster Akiba Rubinstein played him in a game while blindfolded. Sammy lost the game, but Rubinstein exclaimed, "You will be World Champion someday!" After Rubinstein showed Sammy a game in which he had defeated Emanuel Lasker, Sammy showed Rubinstein how he could have won the game in fewer moves.

When he was nine years old Sammy toured Europe, giving exhibition matches in Berlin, Vienna, Paris, London, and other cities. Every place Sammy went, people were interested in the boy chess player who could beat even the best of adult opponents. Sammy remarked, "People stared at me, poked at me, tried to hug me, and asked me questions. Professors measured my cranium and psychoanalyzed me."

In Berlin, Dr. Franziska Baumgarten, a psychologist, examined Sammy. The boy had not had any formal schooling, and he identified pictures of animals poorly. He knew the day of the week, but not the date of the month. In an arithmetic test, Sammy performed below average for his age. But in taking a test to distinguish the shapes of various objects (a test much like putting together a jigsaw puzzle), Sammy performed quite differently. He found the correct answers to many problems considered difficult for children twice his age, and he solved one problem that had never been worked out correctly by any child before. Sammy performed even better on a memory test. He was allowed four minutes to memorize 40 diagrams shown on a piece of paper. After the paper was removed, Sammy redrew the diagrams without a single mistake and in the proper order.

In 1920 Sammy's parents brought him to the United States. Sammy gave a chess exhibition at West Point, where his victory over future military strategists stimulated the public's interest. In 1921 Sammy played in a New York tournament during which former World Champion Emanuel Lasker required 70 moves to beat him.

In spite of these successes, Sammy's days as a chess prodigy were ending. The exhibitions provided much publicity but little money. In 1924 American philanthropist Julius Rosenwald promised to provide for Sammy's future if he would acquire an education. Sammy moved into the house of Morris Steinberg in Detroit, where he was tutored for six months. After passing an entrance examination in 1924, he entered high school.

From 1924 to 1929, Sammy played no professional chess. In fact chess was forbidden to him, except for a couple of occasions during the summer. In 1929 Sammy graduated from high school with "fairly good grades." Two years later he completed his formal education upon receiving a degree in accounting from Chicago University.

Samuel Reshevsky competes with
Danish chess master Bent Larsen.

After not playing competitive chess for many years, Samuel Reshevsky took part in the Western Chess Championship. He won first place easily. Reshevsky continued to perform well in most of the tournaments that followed. Only his lack of knowledge about openings prevented him from doing even better. His excellent defensive skill and endgame technique rescued him from the brink of defeat in game after game.

Chess champion Issac Kashdan wrote in the May 1933 issue of *Chess Review*: "Sammy is at the cross-roads. If he continues in chess, he has every prospect of repeating his triumphs as a child wonder. But as a young man looking for his place in the business world, he would have little time for serious chess playing. The time is at hand when he must choose."

As it turns out, Reshevsky has played an active role in both the worlds of chess and business. From 1933 to 1972, he has carried on the two professions simultaneously. As a result, he has not always done as well as he is capable of in the big international chess tournaments.

Samuel Reshevsky U.S.A — Bent Larsen DENMARK

Reshevsky is a superb blitz player (blitz chess is played with lightning speed, using the shortest possible time for each move). But his reputation stems mainly from his ability to slowly and carefully exploit the smallest advantages. At one time or another, Reshevsky has defeated just about every big name in chess. He has won the United States Chess Championship eight times. In 1972 Reshevsky tied for first place with Robert Byrne and Luborir Kavalek.

There have been other prodigies in chess, and there have been other great masters. But outside of José Capablanca, no prodigy other than Reshevsky has remained a first-rate grandmaster for so many years.

Paul Keres

(1916-   )

Like Alexander Alekhine, Mikhail Botvinnik, and Samuel Reshevsky, Paul Keres came from the old, pre-revolutionary Russia. He was born in the province of Estonia on January 7, 1916. When Keres was four years old, he learned to play chess by watching his father. Before long, he and his older brother were playing the game almost constantly.

At 15, Keres was already a good player and needed only experience to develop his skills. It was difficult for him to play chess seriously in his hometown because he lacked competition. So Keres began playing chess by correspondence. His lively style attracted wide attention. It was in correspondence chess that Keres experimented in making the game as complicated as possible in order to improve his ability as a tactician.

In 1934 Keres won the Estonian Chess Championship, even though he was the youngest of the competitors in the event. This important win qualified him to play in his first international event—the 1935 Chess Olympiad in Warsaw, Poland. Keres came to the tournament as an unknown and was thought to have little chance of distinguishing himself. To the surprise of many, however, Keres had an excellent showing and earned 12 points out of a possible 19. The following year he and Alexander Alekhine tied for first place in a tournament at Bad Nauheim, Germany. In 1937 Keres was invited to take part in the Grand Master Tournament at Semmering, Austria. José Capablanca and Samuel Reshevsky were favored to win, but Keres shocked everyone by forging into an early lead and clinching first place with three rounds to go.

Paul Keres plays for the U.S.S.R. in a match against Svetozar Gligoric of Yugoslavia.

Probably the greatest achievement of Keres' life came in 1938 at the A.V.R.O. Tournament in Holland. Keres tied for first place in the tournament, finishing ahead of World Champion Alekhine and former World Champions José Capablanca and Max Euwe. This triumph made Keres the logical choice to challenge Alekhine for the World Championship, but Keres felt that he was not mature enough. In 1940, however, he proposed that a match be held between himself and Alekhine. Unfortunately, World War II broke out, and the match never took place.

Paul Keres belongs to a select group of chess players who, at the height of their power, were stronger than the official World Champion. No other person has come closer to becoming World Champion without making it than Keres. Four times he has finished second in the Candidates' Tournament. If Keres had won any of these tournaments, he would have qualified to play in the World Chess Championship.

Although he has never won the world title, Keres is certainly one of the top chess players in the world. A fierce attacking player, he possesses a genius for combinations as well as great knowledge of chess theory and positional techniques. In 1962 Keres was honored for his brilliant playing when he was named "Sportsman of the Year" in the U.S.S.R.

Keres claims that he has given up hope of becoming World Champion, but he continues to play frequently in tournaments. And one can always count on him to finish at or near the top in every event in which he competes.

Mikhail Tal

(1936-   )

Former World Champion Mikhail Tal was born in Riga, the capital of Latvia, in 1936 (Latvia became part of the U.S.S.R. in 1940). Many players believe that when Tal is playing at his best, he has no equal. Certainly, Tal's magnificient performances between 1957 and 1960 support this belief. Lately, however, a serious kidney disease has prevented the Soviet chess star from playing as well as he can.

As a small boy, Mikhail enjoyed playing hide-and-go-seek. But when Mikhail was eight, his older cousin taught him how to play a new game—chess. Mikhail liked the game, and he soon joined the chess club of the Young Pioneers, a youth organization. He played in many tournaments and improved his game rapidly. In 1953 Tal enjoyed his first important victory by placing first in the Latvian Chess Championship. Four years later, he graduated from the University of Riga, majoring in history and philosophy.

From 1957 to 1960, Mikhail Tal played chess better than anyone else in the world. For a time, it seemed as if the talented young player was unbeatable. After winning the Soviet Chess Championship in 1957, Tal went on to win the same event in 1958 and 1959. Then, in 1960, Mikhail Tal became the new World Chess Champion by defeating the great Mikhail Botvinnik. That same year, the Latvian magazine *Sports* named Tal "Athlete of the Year."

In 1961 Tal's kidney disease worsened, and Tal's playing suffered as a result. Against his doctors' advice, Tal
decided to defend his title against Mikhail Botvinnik in the
1961 World Chess Championship. In his weakened condi-
tion, he was badly defeated by Botvinnik. (Many chess
devotees still believe that if Tal had not been ill, he would
have won the event.)

Tragedy struck Tal again in 1962—this time at the
Candidates' Tournament in Curacao, an island in the West
Indies. Tal had undergone a major kidney operation just
two months before the tournament, and he played poorly.
Halfway through the tournament, he was hospitalized for
medical tests. Tal wanted to play his remaining games from
his hospital bed, but the tournament officials would not
permit it. While Tal was hospitalized, the only contestant
who visited him was Bobby Fischer—the famous U.S.
player known more for his bad temper than for his kindness.

Although Tal's star has descended, his playing is still
legendary. Some observers claim that Tal stares at his
opponents between moves to hypnotize them. But if any-
thing "hypnotizes" his opponents, it is Tal's brilliant playing. Tal plays chess boldly and imaginatively, and he loves

combinations. Because he frequently attempts combinations even when he cannot foresee a clear result, his games often teeter on the edge of disaster. But Tal doesn't mind taking risks—he plays to win.

Since 1960, Tal has been plagued almost continuously by ill health. Nevertheless, he has made it to the Candidates' Tournament three times—in 1962, 1965, and 1967—since losing the world title to Botvinnik. Mikhail Tal is not old. In fact, he is younger than many of the current grandmasters. If he recovers from his kidney disease, Tal may well prove that he is still the best chess player in the world.

Boris Spassky

(1937-   )

Boris Spassky was born in Leningrad on January 30, 1937. In 1941, when Leningrad was besieged by the Germans, he was evacuated to Moscow, where he spent the war years. He had learned chess at the age of five, and in 1946, back in Leningrad, he joined the chess club of the Young Pioneers. He often cried and became angry when he lost a game.

In 1947 Boris was awarded a special prize for playing the best game in the Russian Federation Junior Championship. Years later he said of himself that at an early age he played like an old man, meaning that his chess was positional and without risks. Spassky's explanation of his mature behavior was that he became the head of his family at age six or seven because his mother was unable to work as a result of a back injury and his father was seldom home.

At 11, he finished fifth in the Leningrad Junior Championship and second in the Russian Federation Junior Championship. Boris found that sound strategy and sacrifices were not quite enough; speculative attack and creativity were also required.

From 1946 to 1950, Boris played chess five hours a day. He was recognized as a chess prodigy, but he also had other interests: history and mathematics in school and, outside, theater, music, and sports. At Leningrad University he began as a math major but switched to journalism because the demands of math interfered with his chess. He was always an excellent student.

In 1966 Bobby Fischer competed against Boris Spassky in the International Grandmaster Chess Tournament and lost.

In 1955 he became the youngest international grand-master, won the World Junior Championship, placed third in the U.S.S.R. Championship, and represented the U.S.S.R. in the Interzonal Tournament at Göteborg—the beginning of the World Championship qualifying cycle.

In 1960 Spassky fell out of favor with the Soviet Chess Federation, probably because of his poor performance in the 1960 World Students' Championship in Leningrad. Playing on board one, he lost his game in only 29 moves to the American William Lombardy—the man who later became a Catholic priest and Bobby Fischer's second in the great 1972 World Championship meet. The United States won the tournament. It was said that Spassky had not trained properly and had failed to take practice sessions seriously. If a Russian chess master "misbehaves," he is suspended from playing abroad for a year. So Boris was not on the U.S.S.R. student team that won in Helsinki in 1961. And, at the last minute, he was replaced at a tournament in Hastings, England.

In spite of being grounded, Spassky won the Russian Chess Championship in 1961. Four years later he won the Candidates' Tournament, thus qualifying to challenge Tigran Petrosian for the world title. He lost that match but not his determination to try again. By winning the Candidates' Tournament in 1968, he qualified for the World Championship play in 1969. This time he defeated Petrosian and became the new World Champion.

In 1972 came the "chess match of the century"— Spassky, age 35, vs. Fischer, age 29. Both had been chess prodigies. Boris held the record of being the youngest international grandmaster at 18. Bobby broke that record by accomplishing the same feat at 15. Until 1972, Spassky had never lost a game to Fischer.

The results of this superpublicized and historic match are well known. Spassky put up a good fight but actually won only two games outright. He is a defeated champion but still one of the greatest and most highly respected players of his time. He will long be remembered for his

World Champion Boris Spassky competing in the Alexander Alekhine Memorial Chess Tournament, 1971

dignity during the trial. His chess life has reached the extremes—brilliant victories to contrast with embarrassing defeats. Still, Spassky may follow in the footsteps of two former Russian titleholders—Alexander Alekhine and Mikhail Botvinnik—and recapture the world title. Certainly, Boris Spassky cannot be counted out as a future contender for the World Championship.

Robert James Fischer

(1943-   )

The greatest player chess has ever known may be a young man born in Chicago on March 9, 1943. His father, a biophysicist, and his mother, a physician, were divorced when their son was very young. The boy, Bobby Fischer, and his sister Joan were brought up by their mother, who took the family from Chicago to California, to Arizona, and finally to Brooklyn, where they settled.

When Bobby was 6, the 11-year-old Joan taught him how to play chess. He became so involved with the game that his mother wrote a letter to a newspaper asking if anyone knew of a child Bobby's age with whom he could play. Herman Helms, the late columnist, suggested that Bobby attend a chess exhibition being given by Max Pavey at the Grand Army Plaza in Brooklyn. Carmine Nigro, president of the Brooklyn Chess Club, was impressed by the youngster and asked him to join his club.

Bobby's first tournament results were not exciting. When he was 12, he came in 20th out of 26 players in the U.S. Junior Open Championship. But one year later, he not only won that same tournament but placed fourth in the U.S. Open. In 1957 Bobby, age 14, won the U.S. Junior, the U.S. Open, and the U.S. Championship, and thereby qualified for the 1958 Interzonal Tournament. By placing fifth in the Interzonal, he became the youngest international grandmaster in history. The next year, at 16, he dropped out of Erasmus Hall High School in Brooklyn so that he could devote all his time to chess.

In 1962 at the Interzonal event in Stockholm, Fischer achieved one of his greatest triumphs. He came in first by two and a half points and qualified for the Candidates' Tournament. However, in this event, he could do no better than fourth place. Fischer blamed his failure on Soviet collusion and accused the Russians of consulting each other during games and agreeing to early draws to save energy. Others said he played poorly because he wore himself out trying to win drawn endgames.

Fourteen-year-old Bobby Fischer makes one of the moves that helped him win the U.S. Open Chess Championship in 1957.

Later that year, Fischer played Botvinnik for the first time at the Chess Olympiad in Varna. Bobby drew that game after obtaining a winning position. He accused Botvinnik of cheating, but no one on the United States team supported him.

It was after these experiences that Fischer was to repeat over and over again that the Russians, while having more top players than all the rest of the world, were not doing much for the game of chess. He thought that they had it in for him especially. The fact that their best players were well paid by the government as professional people whereas he, Fischer, was poor—living out of a suitcase in hotel rooms much of the time—and that the Russians could obtain much better playing experience than he, only served to spur him on. Fischer was going to lead a one-man crusade to show that he could outperform them all. It would be one man against an entire system. Another David was going to take on another giant.

In 1968, despite pleas from the U.S. State Department, Fischer, in first place by a wide margin, left the Interzonal Tournament in Tunisia after a wrangle involving adjourned games.

After playing comparatively little serious chess for two years, he entered the match of the World vs. the U.S.S.R. Playing on board two, he was opposed by former World Champion Tigran Petrosian. Many thought that Fischer would be out of shape, but he trounced Petrosian decisively with a score of three to one. As expected the Russians won the contest, but Fischer's triumph electrified the chess world.

Fischer wanted to compete as a United States representative in the 1970 Interzonal meet. But only the top three finishers from the United States Chess Championship could enter. Although Fischer had won that championship eight times, once with a perfect score, he had not played in the recent matches because his demand that the event be enlarged to 22 rounds instead of the usual 11 had not been met. When, however, third-place finisher Pal Benko, an international grandmaster, heard from Colonel Edmundson of the U.S. Chess Federation that Fischer might be interested in trying again for the world title, he immediately agreed to step down. In the Interzonal, Bobby took first place by a whopping three and a half points, winning his last seven games outright, and qualified for the Candidates' Tournament. In May 1971 he played Mark Taimanov in Vancouver, British Columbia, and made history by winning with a score of six to nothing. No international grandmaster had ever lost by that score. Next came the match with Bent Larsen in Denver in July 1971. Again Fischer won by an incredible six to nothing. In September 1971 the last obstacle to the World Championship match began. Fischer played Tigran Petrosian again in Buenos Aires. Winning the first game gave him an unbelievable 20 in a row. The final outcome was Fischer six and a half, Petrosian two and a half. Petrosian won only one game—the second—and drew three. Hence, Fischer achieved one goal: he qualified to play the chess champion of the world.

The championship match of the century, Fischer vs. Spassky, was to begin early in the summer of 1972, but a lot was to happen before a single game was played and an almost unheard of city was to become a household word.

Receiving offers from many cities to sponsor the chess meet and going over lists of choices from Spassky and Fischer, the International Chess Federation scheduled the championship to begin June 22 and to be played in two countries: the first half in Yugoslavia, and the second half in Iceland.

Fischer was dissatisfied with the prize offered; so the Belgrade organizers, fearing that he would not show up, demanded that the U.S. Chess Federation advance a $35,000 guarantee for his appearance. The Soviet Union agreed to a guarantee for Spassky, but the U.S. Chess Federation did not have the money, could not, and would not make a financial guarantee for any chess player. Yugoslavia withdrew its bid to play host. As a result, the entire match was rescheduled to begin in Reykjavik, Iceland, on July 2.

Convinced that chess deserved better playing conditions and a greater financial reward, Fischer pressed for different arrangements. The International Chess Federation answered by giving him four days to either accept the conditions or forfeit his chance at the world title. Many people wrote and called Fischer, asking him to reconsider his decision. Nine hours before the deadline, Presidential Adviser Henry Kissinger appealed to his patriotism in an attempt to persuade him to play.

A few days before the match was to begin, Fischer caused another uproar by repeating his demand for more money. He said that if the purse, which stood at an all-time high of $125,000 was not increased, he would not play. Still holding out, Fischer failed to show up in Reykjavik for the opening day. Suddenly, British financier James Slater, no mean chess player himself, offered a dazzling $125,000 donation to the championship purse. Slater wrote, "If he isn't afraid of Spassky, then I, Jim Slater, have removed the element of money." Fischer set out for the World Championship.

He arrived in Iceland two days late. Angered and insulted, World Champion Spassky demanded a written apology from him. Fischer apologized for his "disrespectful behavior." After more postponements granted first to Fischer and then to Spassky, the first game of the 1972 World Chess Championship finally began on July 11. Spassky's second was Yefim Geller, a Soviet grandmaster who had won more games from Fischer than anyone else in the world. Fischer's second was Father William Lombardy.

Fischer lost the first game. On the 29th move, he made a blunder—perhaps the worst in his career. Ordinarily, Fischer is the master of precise play and makes fewer mistakes than others. Were the distractions from all the hassles on getting the match started too much? Maybe someday he will answer the question.

Before the second game was to begin, Fischer demanded that the television cameras be removed. The request was turned down as contrary to the original agreements. He locked himself in his room while Spassky sat embarrassed in the playing hall and won by forfeit.

Fischer arrives in Iceland for the 1972 World Chess Championship.

Fischer down by two games! Could that be true? Was he overrated? Where was all the "Fischer-fear" that usually froze opposing players? Could he really go home as he threatened after waiting years for this match? Fischer had been saying for a long time that he was the best chess player in the world. What about all the money Slater put up? He simply had to stay and fight. Lina Grumette, a friend from Los Angeles with a son his age, talked with Fischer for five hours to comfort him. John Collins, Fischer's early chess teacher from Brooklyn, now in a wheelchair, played chess with him all night to calm him. His sister Joan flew to Reykjavik. Spassky went fishing.

Father Lombardy asked Lothar Schmid, the referee, to hold the third game in a small room behind the stage and to use closed-circuit television. Schmid called Spassky. Always a decent person, and feeling guilty about winning the second game by forfeit, Spassky agreed.

Playing black, Fischer won the third game, his first win over Spassky. In spite of this victory, Fischer continued to make newspaper headlines with his insistent requirements for better lighting, removal of television cameras, and elimination of noise from front-row spectators. Even so, he outplayed Spassky in the openings, the middles, and the endgames. As Spassky fought for his life, the Russians, but not Spassky, made fantastic claims—all unsupported—that Fischer was using electronic and chemical aids.

After the second game, Spassky got only one more win. Eleven games were drawn. Fischer won seven to make the final score Fischer 12½, Spassky 8½. Bobby Fischer became the first American World Chess Champion. A Russian had held the title since 1948.

What kind of personality is part of an individual with a brilliant mind who focuses on chess before the age of 10, quits high school because it is not advancing his chess, lives in hotels and small apartments, and has little or no social life? Clues to the answer might be found by comparing Fischer with Isaac Newton. Both grew up without fathers in the household and were loners with high principles. They were difficult to get along with. Fischer said, "They call me temperamental, but I am not. I don't go out of my way to look for trouble." Newton could have said the same thing—no one wanted more to avoid personal arguments.

Nevertheless, he often had such arguments, some of which received worldwide attention. Their personal lives and careers were one. Psychiatrists say that suspicious people do not lie. A few years ago, when asked who he thought was the strongest chess player in the world, Fischer gave a Muhammed-Ali kind of reply, "It is nice to be modest, but it would be stupid if I did not tell the truth. It is Fischer." Was this bragging? Probably not. Fischer had to tell the truth as he saw it. No matter what one says about their unpleasant behavior, Newton's and Fischer's accomplishments resulted from a rare combination of unusual talent plus hard work done mostly without the help of others.

Babe Ruth's personality and talents as a home-run king, hitter, and pitcher made baseball what it is today. Bobby Fischer has done the same for chess. Near the end of the World Chess Championship, *Pravda*, the major newspaper in the U.S.S.R., reported the match in one small paragraph on an inside page, while in the United States, chess was making headlines. This sudden change, this new excitement, not to mention the better playing conditions, higher fees, increased prestige, and even the newer rules for matches—all are due to Fischer. He alone has set these high standards, and others must now meet them.

GAMES	1	2	3	4	5	6	7	8	9	10	11	12	13	14	15	16	17	18	19	20	21	TOTAL
Spassky	1	1	0	½	0	0	½	0	½	0	1	½	0	½	½	½	½	½	½	½	0	8½
Fischer	0	0	1	½	1	1	½	1	½	1	0	½	1	½	½	½	½	½	½	½	1	12½

The scores for the 1972 World Chess Championship. As the challenger to World Champion Spassky, Bobby Fischer needed 12½ points to win the title, while Spassky needed only 12 points to retain it. The World Championship match can last up to 24 games, but Fischer gained the 12½ points he needed to win after only 21 games.

the author

It seemed only natural for Peter M. Lerner to write a book about chess and chess players, for he learned the game as a teenager and has been an enthusiastic player ever since. In 1971 he won the New England Junior Chess Championship. Peter Lerner founded and captained the chess teams at Amity High School in Woodbridge, Connecticut, and at Washington and Jefferson College, where he is a pre-law student.

The Pull Ahead Books

AMERICA'S FIRST LADIES
  1789 to 1865

AMERICA'S FIRST LADIES
  1865 to the Present Day

DARING SEA CAPTAINS

DOERS AND DREAMERS

FAMOUS CHESS PLAYERS

FAMOUS CRIMEFIGHTERS

FAMOUS SPIES

INDIAN CHIEFS

PIRATES AND BUCCANEERS

POLITICAL CARTOONISTS

PRESIDENTIAL LOSERS

SINGERS OF THE BLUES

STARS OF THE ZIEGFELD FOLLIES

WESTERN LAWMEN

WESTERN OUTLAWS

We specialize in publishing quality books for young people. For a complete list please write

Lerner Publications Company

241 First Avenue North, Minneapolis, Minnesota 55401